PACK UP AND AND PAINT

Landscapes

Tom Robb

SELECT
EDITIONS

CLB 4435

Published 1995 by CLB Publishing
Exclusively for Selectabook Ltd, Devizes
© 1995 CLB Publishing, Godalming, Surrey

ISBN 1-85833-341-5

All rights reserved. No part of this publication
may be reproduced, stored in a retrieval
system, or transmitted in any form or by any
means, electronic, mechanical, photocopying,
recording, or otherwise, without the prior
written permission of the copyright owner.

Printed and bound in Hong Kong

Introduction

Once you decide to explore the world of outdoor painting, your first goal is likely to be a trip to the country, or even to a large park – anywhere you can find a sense of space, trees on the horizon and a feeling of being in touch with nature. These are the traditional sources and inspiration for landscape painting, and luckily most of us are within reasonably easy reach of some place that will supply them.

In the first part of this book, you'll find help in putting together the right kind of equipment for the trips you want to make. There are also hints on how to plan your trip, where to go and so on.

I've tried to suggest a few of the pitfalls and perplexities as well as the positive aspects. You will soon discover that there is so much to look at, for instance, and so many things to paint that the real problem will be choosing a viewpoint or an interesting angle.

I also include some useful techniques, and an array of seasonal colour codes to help you realise how much your palette changes with the weather and temperature. And finally, I offer you three projects to set you a real challenge, no matter what level of experience you have.

Creating an individual way of painting the landscape in all its wonderful diversity must be the goal of every outdoor artist. This handbook has been planned to make it as simple and straightforward as possible; I hope it will also become a useful companion as you Pack Up And Paint.

Tom Robb

Contents

Tom Robb

Why landscapes?

Landscape painting is a language for our habitat. Its
vocabulary is made up of leaves, trees, earth, sky and stone;
its grammar is in the way these are put together in patterns.
And the patterns that we can see in the landscape can be
read by any human being in a hundred different ways.

As soon as you decide to try painting a landscape –
especially if you are going to paint out of doors – you
are already asking yourself questions about what you in
particular are seeing, and why you want to share that vision.

What is there about a landscape that affects us all so much,
and that creates so many emotional reactions? A part of the
answer is familiarity. We live on the planet earth, where we
are surrounded by an environment of growing plants. Even
those of us who have never seen a simple stretch of
farmland, a wooded pool or the rolling contours of hill and
moorland, will have seen something of nature's power in
films or in wildlife programmes on television.

Fed on a diet of in-depth studies and documentaries filmed
in remote archipelagos, it may take an effort to relate these
exotic places to our more mundane surroundings, but you
can transfer some of the increased knowledge and
appreciation they bring to your own home ground.

The countryside excels in a kind of 'atmospheric talent' – a
golden moment of tranquillity one day; a dramatic
overpowering mountain landscape on another. A clump of
nearby trees is all you can see in the early morning – until
the mist lifts to reveal a far-flung panorama that seems to go
on to the ends of the earth.

Above all, the landscape is our territory. We fight over it,
build on it, dream about it and sometimes die for it. More,
perhaps, than any other subject in art, it involves us all. The
painter of the countryside will always find a welcoming
audience as well as tremendous personal enjoyment.

Practical planning

What you will need

Planning your outing is essential if you are to make the best use of your time and energy. The mediums and the specific problems that each one brings are covered in the first books of this series. Here I'd like to mention just a few of the pitfalls that have entrapped me or my students during painting trips to various country sites, as well as some of the sensible hints that have proved their worth over many years.

It is impossible, of course, to be dogmatic about what you might need, because the terrain and the weather conditions vary so much from place to place and time to time.

Start with clothing. Make sure that what you wear is loose enough to be comfortable and old enough to be disposable if necessary. Painting is not a fashion show, and it can demand surprising spurts of energy, sending you scrambling through ditches, hedges or sandy dunes to reach the site with a perfect view – always just over the next hill, or down the next valley.

Trousers or a longish skirt will keep away the worst of the scratches and mosquito bites; sun-tan oil will keep your face, neck and hands from burning. I make a habit of looking for places where I can stand with my back to the sun. It's better for the painting, too, as the light falls over your shoulder on to the canvas or paper.

Wandering through fields is likely to be muddy no matter what the time of year, so keep rubber boots in your car. If you don't drive, carry a pair of light plastic shoes that fit over your own – not very sturdy, but they make up for it in convenience.

A vacuum flask of hot or cold drink and a packet of sandwiches are vital; once you settle down to paint you won't want to keep stopping and starting. Sometimes I take along a small radio to add a little background music, or to help keep track of the time.

And don't forget the compass. It's all too easy to get lost even in this crowded country. I have made quite a few trips when I couldn't find the car, or even the road where I left it, before I learned to carry one with me all the time.

A good map is also essential; keep one just for painting trips, and mark the places you like so you can find them again. And binoculars are a great help – for doing a spot of bird-watching or, more to the point, for bringing a distant building or tree into focus so that you can get some idea of its detail.

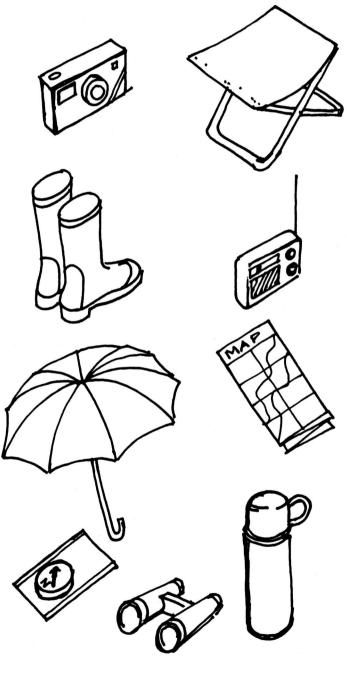

Making the most of it

And now for the painting tools themselves:

I usually carry an easel on landscape outings. I enjoy painting out of doors, and I like to do as much as I can on the site rather than carry sketches home to develop in the studio. My 'touring' easel is an old wooden one, but the new aluminium models with telescopic legs are ideal.

The medium I use depends a great deal on the time of year. You'll find greatly expanded notes with the seasonal colour codes on pages 26-43. But you should always begin with the minimum that you think you will need rather than the maximum. Making the most of your equipment is a good way to learn its possibilities and its limitations.

If you plan to be drawing and you want to try out a variety of papers, it's not necessary to carry three or four separate pads; tear off a few sheets from each and staple them together to make a notebook. You might try taking just three or four pastels and three or four pencils or pens in the same colours, to see how different the results can be on the same paper.

Watercolour paints are easier to carry than oils; you need only take a box and a single brush, plus some kind of water supply. Using only one brush, of course, means washing it all the time to keep your colours clean.

An easel and board are still a great advantage, but if you really want to travel light, find a place where you can prop the board or even a single piece of cardboard backing against a support. This should be absolutely firm; otherwise, the brush may push the paper around, making you lose control of the effect you are aiming for.

But don't stint on the paper. You can carry a pre-stretched pad, so you don't need boards or masking tape; but even on an outing to make a single sketch, use the best paper you can find. Then make sure you let it work for you.

This sketch was done in a clearing of a forest. The trunks of the trees are not painted at all: the paper comes through as part of the painting, not simply as a surface.

Exploring the ways in which paper and paint can work actively *with* you is one of the great pleasures of painting.

Where to go

Happily for the landscape painter, the countryside is filled with interesting places to see and to sketch. But it will work best for you when you have thought out carefully in advance what kind of painting you want to do that day, and what sort of effect you hope to achieve.

For example, if you have been making sketches of long, low hills, you might like to try something more vertical. Mountains can't always be had to order, but there are other ways of adding a vertical line to your view. Look for a church spire; many country villages have churches that can be seen far across the hills, and they will provide the necessary focus.

Or try getting near to a rise in the ground, and then painting sitting down instead of standing up. Just those few feet of change in eye level can make the hill loom up in front of you. And if you have been painting fields of growing crops, try walking through woodland for a change, and see what the vertical effect of trees can do to your composition.

Travelling to new places should bring you new views to paint. Keep an eye on the paintability of scenes and landscapes whenever you stray from your usual route. Maybe just walking down a different road will bring all sorts of changes to the colours and the shapes of familiar fields.

And even a few clustered trees can become a forest if you are near enough to them. Don't be afraid to work close up. Most of us tend to look for the far-reaching vista, forgetting that a glimpse through a garden gate or down an allotment path can be just as exciting to paint, and perhaps even more interesting to look at afterwards.

If all else fails, and you are caught out in the open on a miserable cloudy day when you can't see further than your easel, don't despair. Make a study of different tree barks in pencil or pen and ink. They are not only marvellously varied and intricate, but will teach you a great deal about how individual species grow and develop. Learning how to capture the way a branch grows out of a trunk will help you to sketch a tree even when the model isn't there in front of you.

Setting up

One of the most confusing and difficult problems for the beginner is finding an appropriate place to set up your painting gear in the depth of the country. You have glimpsed a glorious view from your car or your bike; there are marvellous scenic moments of beauty around every corner, and you promise yourself to come back and paint there the very next day.

Well, the next day turns into the next month – or the next season. You're not quite sure of the exact spot, and nothing looks the same. When you finally stop and try to set up your gear, you find that the verge hides a deep and muddy ditch which is impossible to cross. So you search for the farmer's field gate (he will have filled in the ditch to let his tractors through), but once across you are confronted with an impenetrable hedge in front of you, the ditch in back of you and nowhere to go but into the field itself. And that is now a sea of mud around the edges, and broken stubble where once the golden rape glittered in the sunlight ...

First and foremost, when you see a place that looks like a landscape you would like to paint, stop and explore. Walk to various vantage points to ascertain the best view; check out the accessibility of the road or footpath; look for somewhere to park your car or your bicycle that will still be available later in the year, and make a careful note of the location. No matter how good your memory, you are unlikely to remember the exact spot, and that one note can save you hours of fruitless tramping.

When you have finally found your 'perfect' view, take the time to set up your painting gear properly. Everything should be to hand, within easy reach.

There is an accepted way of putting out your colours on the palette, working from yellows, ochres, reds, browns, greens, blues to black. Frankly, this is simply a way of making it easy to dip your brush in the right spot without coming to grief. It does make it easier, but it is not an iron rule. What is most important is for your own arrangement to be consistent.

Place your jug of water or cup of turpentine in the same place every time you paint. It really does stop you from suddenly realizing that you've been overlaying that pale blue sky with tea or coffee. When you are concentrating, anything out of the ordinary can be a source of interruption.

On your way to your site, look around for an empty cardboard box – something small and light that will keep your bits and pieces off the ground, prop up your brushes and make a convenient waste bin when you are finished. If you have a car, keep such a box handy in the boot.

But do ask before you take anything, as you should also ask permission to set up on private land. Most of the countryside does belong to someone, even if it looks completely deserted. So don't leave litter or open gates behind you; this will not only make you unwelcome on another occasion, but it will also make it difficult for other painters who follow you.

Choosing what to paint

The old proverb that says it is better to travel than to arrive holds a great deal of truth for the landscape painter. Sometimes we forget how much real pleasure is involved in choosing what to paint.

Finally, there you are, set up and ready to go in front of an amazing vista. Where on earth, literally, do you begin? A beautiful view does not necessarily make an interesting composition. Masses and masses of green, especially when it is all of the same species, can be very dull.

You need to look for scale and focus, The most interesting pictures have something in the foreground, something in the middle and something in the distance.

Remember that two out of three is a good start. If you have a pleasant field of corn in the middle distance and a tree-topped hill in the background, you can try moving a gate-post or an arching shrub to the foreground. If there is a richly coloured tree just by your spot, and a lovely line of distant fields away on the horizon, a small farmhouse 'transplanted' from a nearby field might just fit the bill for the middle distance, dropping into place with a red roof to give it additional visibility.

The sketch here, made near the sea, was simply to see if the boat masts rising up over the hills looked too strange to be part of the painting, In the end, I decided that without more detail, they would look extremely strange indeed, and so the masts became trees! An alternative would have been to walk up the hill towards the boats until a little of their shape and form, as well as their masts, was visible.

Finding something different

Unusual objects

Another important point about choosing interesting
subjects is to remind yourself how many extraordinary
things there are in the landscape – and not all of them by
any means natural. People are great builders, and especially
prolific when it comes to adding decoration and
ornamentation.

Even when the landscape is dark and gloomy, or it's too
cold to spend a long time out in the fields, there are
hundreds of unusual objects to draw and paint. Farm
buildings and farmyards, for instance, are always filled with
strange shapes and curious items of equipment.

Textures of wood and stone make good exercises for the
landscape painter. You'll need to be able to put them into
your paintings sooner or later, and once you know how to
portray them, the knowledge will be there even when you
don't have the image in front of you.

It is especially enjoyable to paint something different. This
lovely stone pineapple, the age-old symbol of hospitality,
stood beside the gate of an ordinary little house in a village.
Perhaps it was taken from a grander place, or perhaps the
little house had once been the lodge to a manor.

In any case, there it was, and getting the shadows of the
carving precise enough to show the crisp outlines, as well as
the way they grew lighter towards the top where the sun hit
the stone directly, took me quite a long time.

There are so many chances of finding something as curious
and paintable as my pineapple that you should always carry
a sketch-book with you, even when you start out with the
intention of painting in oil. I get distracted by this
sometimes; that's a danger whenever you go out to paint,
but moderation in all things.

Understanding how something is made can be the best way
of learning how to show what it looks like with the
minimum of fuss and bother. Once your hand knows the
feeling of solidity of this pineapple, for example, you'll be
able to set it on its pillar far away in the landscape with no
more than the flick of a brush.

Interesting people

This sketch shows why it is important to make your own drawings rather than to rely entirely on photographs for your details.

Studying the way people move and sit out in the open is quite different from painting them in the studio. You are not at all interested in their features or in the particulars of their clothes, but simply in the way they would appear as participants in the drama of the landscape that you want to paint.

Find a comfortable seat outside a country pub, in the window of a village tea-shop or beside the gate of a farm. This isn't the same as a city scene. Everyone will be more settled; they will move more slowly, and the quiet solidity of their appearance should be reflected in the strokes you use. No upward flicks or figures leaning forward as they hurry to the station.

Don't worry about colour. I used chalk here, but any kind of pastel or watercolour wash would do. Thin oil paint works well, too, but you'll need a little more paraphernalia, and sometimes that makes your subjects self-conscious.

Keep the outlines simple and your brush or chalk light. It's the feeling of spontaneity you want to achieve. Look for the things that catch your eye – the brim of a hat, the line of a cane, the heaviness of the bench.

Practise this kind of sketching as often as you can. When people move about, their bodies form many different shapes, so even if you are watching one person, you can end up with a whole page of drawings.

Keep these drawings as references for when you need additions to your paintings. A scene by a mill might be made a little more interesting with a miller tipping the flour fresh-ground from the wheel, or carrying sacks into the store.

A drawing of a village street would look much more lively if there were a number of people moving about and chatting. You might actually be there on early-closing day, when there isn't a person in sight, but with your notebook to hand – hey presto! – the population grows immediately.

Techniques

Working quickly

There are two different approaches to landscapes, the quick
sketch and the slow, contemplative painting, and each has
its place in your vocabulary of techniques.

When you are out of doors, conditions are likely to change
very quickly and it is vital to be able to switch from thinking
a long time about a painting, studying the view from
different angles and setting up an elaborate 'camp', only to
be brought swiftly out of your preoccupation by a clap of
thunder and a deluge of rain that makes it impossible to do
more than run for shelter.

And the weather is not your only problem. We tend to think
that the landscape is something that stays put year after year,
to which we can return at will. Indeed, we often go looking
for the landscapes of centuries ago, in the 'footsteps' of great
painters, hoping to find the very spot from which Constable,
for example, might first have seen Flatford Mill.

But landscape changes constantly with light and climatic
conditions. It is seldom the same for more than a few hours.
So it is important to learn to do quick sketches that are more
than simply outlines and colour notes. These should have
enough of the painterly about them to be satisfactory in
themselves.

Once you steel yourself to a schedule of ten to fifteen
minutes at the most, you'll be amazed at what you can
produce in the time. There will be a feeling of freshness and
spontaneity that is hard to achieve in any other way. Aside
from being a record of what a particular place looked like at
a particular time, you may well find that you have a
delightful painting in its own right, despite – or perhaps
even because of – the speed.

Don't imagine that quick notes have to be in pencil or
watercolour, although both are simple to use. Very thin oil
paint is also effective, with a rag to brush the colour away, as
Turner used to do.

The details here are from an oil sketch I made, recording
the changing colour of the bark, the clouds and the sky.

Working slowly

Every moment in a landscape can bring something new; one day's meadow is tomorrow's newly ploughed field.

After I had settled down to paint one morning, the view down this allotment lane was completely obscured when the gardener in the right-hand hut wished me a pleasant good morning, opened the door to his shed, and proceeded to move machinery and tools out of the hut for a full hour. So while the shed door was open, I tried different ways of sketching the trees.

At the allotment, the shapes and sizes of the huts attracted me particularly, for they made an unusual subject. I'd suggest that any landscape painter look for places like that. Working areas often have an air of purpose about them which is salutary after weeks of wide vistas and empty countryside.

The shadows moved quite a lot while I was working; by the time I had finished, the sun was overhead and the shadows had gone completely. But the quick sketch I had done at the beginning showed exactly where the shadows had been, and I painted them in appropriately. It is far better to make that kind of preliminary drawing to use as a reference than to try to finish the painting itself too quickly.

This is a complex scene, with all kinds of lines and subtle colours to incorporate into the main design of the path stretching away in front of me. But such paintings are well worth the trouble they take.

Working slowly gives you the chance to think about what you are doing, to look carefully so that you paint what you actually see, rather than what theoretical rules of perspective might suggest.

Oil is a good medium, because it stays flexible long enough for you to continue making changes as you work.

Always try to alternate quick sketching days with days in which you allow yourself enough time for careful and considered painting.

The four seasons colour codes

A marvellous discovery is in store for you when you begin
to look analytically at landscapes. The range of colour that is
revealed to the discerning eye is truly remarkable.

Although I have grouped colour codes by the season, there
are, of course, many more variations from month to month,
week to week and even day to day. As the autumn leaves
turn, for example, they go through a dozen separate colour
changes, from palest spring yellow to wintery brown-black.

You will see that the colour codes are made up from
relatively few basic pigments. They indicate how much
variety you can get with only a few tubes or pans of paint,
and make it clear that you need not carry huge boxes full of
every shade the colourmen ever invented.

The names for oil and watercolour paints are often the
same, but they look entirely different.

For the first-time painter, the codes can literally make your
choices for you. If you are fairly advanced, you may find it
useful to compare your paintings with the codes to discover
ways of expanding your range. And if you are genuinely
experienced, it could be both interesting and instructive to
create personal colour codes based on your own
observations, and to tuck them into this book for reference.

The numbers on the colour codes are a guide to mixing.
They are the proportions that I used to work out the charts.
Although they are accurate as far as they go, it is obviously
not like weighing pigments on a scale or using a measuring
spoon.

There can also be variations in a colour of the same name,
depending on the brand of paint you use.

These do not necessarily appear at first, but as you mix the
colour with other pigments, there may be a definite change.
Some makes become darker – yellows, for example, turn
slightly brown; greens become olive in tone.

So try your own paints in the proportions given, and see
how they match up to the colours in the code. If they don't
match, vary the proportions, and if, after that, there are still
considerable differences, experiment with another brand.

The spring palette

Of all the seasons, spring to me is artistically the most
exciting. I imagine that is true for most painters. There is
something about the blossoming trees, the fresh shades of
new leaf green that bring out the romantic in us all.

But spring, surprisingly, has darker colours too – deep
shadows, and hollows in the ground where the winter still
lingers. The weather is far from certain; sometimes, when I
know it is likely to be especially changeable, I take a camera
along for a first quick shot. But it isn't a good idea to depend
upon a photograph instead of your eyes.

The problem is not that it is too easy – I'm all in favour of
making things as easy as possible for yourself – but that the
colour won't be accurate. Until you have the experience to
visualize in paint instead of in film, you can be misled by a
photograph, and your paintings may end up looking like
snapshots.

I like watercolour and pastels best at this time of year, as
both can be easily lightened – with wash for the
watercolour, and layers of white for the pastel on top of the
original colour.

The clearest colours seem the most suitable, and I use most
of the pigments by themselves. There is a great deal of
yellow in everything; greens and pinks are sharp and pure,
and the blue skies of spring have a special translucency that
is truly breathtaking.

Spring evenings can be a problem. The soft purple haze that
we see early in the year is a fugitive colour, and a delicate
hand is needed.

But spring mornings are relatively easy to capture – palest
ochres, paler greens and a few splashes of a yellow wash on
top – and there, you have painted April.

The colour code on the following pages is made up of
watercolours, above, and pastels below. The watercolours
are used with a very light hand, and plenty of water to dilute
the pigment, but there are very few mixtures of colours. The
pastels are almost all just as they come in the box.

Prussian blue 1 Wash 6	Cadmium orange	Burnt umber 1 Wash 6	Viridian green 1 Wash 8	Ivory black 1 Wash 5
Yellow ochre 2 Wash 6	Cobalt blue 1 Wash 3	Raw sienna 1 Wash 6	Lemon yellow 2 Wash 2	Ultramarine blue 1 Viridian green 1 Wash 6
Cobalt blue 3 Raw sienna 1	Ivory black 1 Viridian green 2	Ultramarine blue 1 Wash 3	Viridian green 2	Ultramarine blue 1 Wash 6
Alizarin crimson 1 Cadmium orange 2	Viridian green 3 Cadmium orange 1	Alizarin crimson 1 Wash 6	Alizarin crimson 2 Wash 2	Prussian blue 2 Ivory black 1 Wash 1
Bright green	Cobalt blue	Deep green	Purple	Middle green
Light purple	Cream	Deep orange	Ultramarine blue	Light blue
Rose red	Orange 1 Pink 3	Light purple	Yellow ochre	Deep blue-grey
Orange	Deep pink	Light rose	Lemon yellow	Moss green

The summer palette

With the warmth of summer, the colours grow deeper and richer. All of your pigments can be a little stronger, a little more concentrated than their spring equivalents.

I use a great deal of oil paint during the summer, because the texture and tone seem to suit the atmosphere of hot afternoons and long light evenings. But I make a point of going out with watercolours and pastels now and then, to keep in touch with the way their light and limpid tones can be adapted to the deeper summer palette.

This is a sketch I did for a large oil landscape; as it happens, I far prefer the sketch to the finished painting. Somehow I feel it manages to give the impression of warmth and sunlight even though it has no yellow and there was very little blue sky.

During the summer you will find that the strong colours appear almost intact: cadmium red and orange, viridian green, cobalt blue and so on. There are some mixtures of ochres and greens to give your painting depth.

You can see almost every colour imaginable in a summer garden, and you can ring the changes from brilliant beds of flowers to the sombre greens of Victorian shrubbery.

One of the curious qualities of summer is that crop colours are missing; although, traditionally, harvest time is not until the autumn, the main farming crops are usually in by midsummer, and the fields of a summer landscape can look surprisingly barren and brown.

So it's a good time to make trips a little farther afield. Stately homes and gardens are pleasant places to set up an easel; there is often a vista or some sort of folly that can add visual elegance and surprise to the scene.

Experiment with new challenges by taking your painting equipment on a summer holiday. The scenery and the colours you use are bound to be affected both by the climate and the culture. Seaside towns make wonderful settings, with peeling walls and boats bobbing in the harbour. Mountain passes create spectacular paintings; and lakes are a natural subject for landscapes as well as waterscapes, a double exercise for your skills.

Look at the difference between the spring colour code on the previous two pages and the summer code following this page. I have used many green and yellow mixtures. Oils are above and the much heavier watercolours are below.

Cadmium orange	Cadmium yellow 3 Viridian green 1	Cadmium yellow	Lemon yellow 3 Ultramarine blue 1	Olive green
Viridian green	Viridian green 2 Lemon yellow 2	Viridian green 1 Lemon yellow 3	Cadmium red 2 Olive green 2	Lemon yellow 3 Olive green 1
Viridian green 2 Lemon yellow 2	Viridian green 1 Zinc white 3	Lemon yellow 3 Yellow ochre 1	Cadmium orange 3 Raw sienna 1	Olive green 2 Cadmium orange 2
Cadmium red	Cadmium yellow 3 Olive green 1	Lemon yellow 2 Zinc white 2	Olive green 3 Cadmium red 1	Ultramarine blue, deep
Viridian green 2 Cadmium yellow 2	Yellow ochre 3 Olive green 1	Lemon yellow 3 Ultramarine blue 1	Cobalt blue	Cadmium yellow 3 Ultramarine blue 1
Olive green 2 Cadmium yellow 2	Purple	Olive green 3 Cobalt blue 1	Cadmium orange, deep	Raw sienna 2 Cadmium yellow 2
Olive green	Lemon yellow	Cadmium red	Olive green 2 Lemon yellow 2	Cadmium orange 3 Purple 1
Burnt sienna	Lemon yellow 3 Cobalt blue 1	Ultramarine blue	Cadmium orange	Cadmium orange 3 Purple 1

The autumn palette

With autumn, the landscape becomes a strange combination
of flaming colours and brooding darkness. Ochres and olive
greens predominate, reds are scarlet and burnt crimson,
and underlying everything is the glorious kaleidoscope of
rich fruit and the approach of brown winter.

There is almost no black at all in the landscape, and most of
the pigments are used straight from the tube, with little or
no mixing necessary.

Colours are dark and brilliant. Ochres and golds are used
instead of lemon yellow or white and all the burnt umber
and burnt sienna variations come into their own; nothing
should be painted half-heartedly at this time of year.

The flourish of painting in summer soon grows a little more
cautious as frosty nights and mornings arrive. You will have
to start thinking about gloves and mufflers, and it can
become startlingly cold in spite of brilliant, deep blue skies
and warmth at midday.

Although I paint in watercolours throughout the year, I have
to admit that autumn seems to be best suited to oil – even
though some of the most successful paintings of trees, and
soft autumn mornings of gold and pale blue, have
traditionally been in watercolour. Not pastel, I think, but
that is always a personal choice.

Autumn also seems a good beginning, even though it marks
the end of long summer evenings painting outside.
Something about the crisp air inspires me to sort out my
equipment, get it clean and tidy and think about what I
want to do next year – and the year after that, too.

The colour code on the following pages gives you some
hint of the richer, browner colours which I prefer, in
watercolour above in the colour code, and oils, below.
I've used very little of the bright yellows and greens
characteristic of summer; instead, there are all the sienna,
ochre and burnt tones, quite a few mixed with purple for a
warm effect. Remember that two colours, three at most, are
usually enough to provide you with almost any colour in
the spectrum.

Burnt sienna 3 Purple 1	Olive green	Cobalt blue	Raw sienna 1 Yellow ochre 3	Yellow ochre
Cerulean blue 2 Ivory black 2	Burnt umber 3 Raw sienna 1	Viridian green 3 Yellow ochre 1	Indian red	Burnt umber
Raw sienna	Cerulean blue	Olive green	Viridian green 2 Cadmium orange 2	Olive green 1 Burnt umber 3
Raw umber	Cadmium orange	Viridian green	Burnt umber 1 Cadmium orange 3	Alizarin crimson
Cadmium yellow 3 Olive green 1	Purple 2 Burnt umber 2	Olive green 3	Ultramarine blue	Lemon yellow 2 Olive green 2
Purple 2 Yellow ochre 2	Purple 2 Ultramarine blue 2	Olive green 3 Cobalt blue 1	Lemon yellow 3 Olive green 1	Olive green
Viridian green	Purple 2 Cadmium orange 2	Purple	Lemon yellow 2 Olive green 3	Cadmium red
Burnt umber	Lemon yellow 3 Ultramarine blue 1	Alizarin crimson	Ivory black	Burnt umber 2 Indian red 2

The winter palette

Winter doesn't necessarily mean snow, but it usually means cold weather, icy winds and cool grey light. With or without the snowy scenes of Christmas cards, the season offers such wonderful effects to the landscape painter that it would be a shame to ignore the months of darkness just because it takes a little extra planning to keep yourself warm as well as comfortable.

You'll need to be well wrapped up, but with enough mobility in arms and fingers to be able to paint easily. So take a lesson from the mountain climbers: it is far better to insulate yourself with many thin layers of sweaters and shirts than to wear one inhibitingly thick anorak. Keep your ears warm under a woolly cap, and be sure to protect your eyes.

Because the light is often poor, it may seem unnecessary to worry about sunglasses, but the winter sun can be deceptive, with a glare that you may not even notice until your eyes begin to hurt from the strain of trying to observe. Use the sort of glasses that have a neutral density, like those worn by

sportsmen and mountain climbers. They will filter out the
harsh light, but leave the colours more or less intact.

The painting on this page is a deliberate twin to the
previous autumn painting, to show how two very similar
studies can have very different colour qualities. The blues
are clearer and colder, the fields tinged with grey instead of
yellow. I normally paint in a much wider range of colours.
If you look at the colour code on the following pages, you'll
see many clear blues, pinks, and a few quiet reds. The top
colours are in watercolour with a medium degree of wash,
the bottom colours in oil.

Obviously you'll want to keep your equipment to a
minimum. Oil colours react badly to intense cold; pastels
will crack or crumble; even drawing pens have been known
to leave frozen trails of ink on the page, which will blur as
soon as you bring them into the warmth of a room.
Watercolour is actually the easiest medium to use, so long
as the cold is dry rather than damp. Spirit-based felt-tip
pens are fairly satisfactory, but their colour range can be too
limited for a scene of delicate shades.

Prussian blue 3 Ivory black 1	Cobalt blue Wash	Ultramarine blue Wash	Raw umber Wash	Yellow ochre Wash
Olive green 1 Cobalt blue 3	Alizarin crimson Wash	Viridian green Wash	Prussian blue Wash	Ultramarine blue 3 Yellow ochre 1
Raw umber Wash	Alizarin crimson Wash	Ivory black 2 Cobalt blue 2	Cerulean blue Wash	Venetian red Wash
Viridian green Wash	Ultramarine blue 1 Ivory black 3	Ultramarine blue, deep Wash	Ivory black Wash	Cobalt blue 3 Ivory black 1
Viridian green, deep	Prussian blue 2 Ivory black 2	Prussian blue 2 Zinc white 2	Cobalt blue 3 Lemon yellow 1	Lemon yellow 2 Ivory black 2
Olive green 3 Viridian green 1	Ultramarine blue 3 Ivory black 1	Burnt umber	Purple 3 Titanium white 1	Ultramarine blue, deep
Cobalt blue 2 Zinc white 2	Ivory black 2 Olive green 2	Cobalt blue 1 Zinc white 3	Lemon yellow 2 Mauve 2	Olive green 3 Lemon yellow 1
Ultramarine blue 2 Zinc white 2	Ultramarine blue 3 Titanium white 1	Cerulean blue 3 Indian red 1	Cobalt blue 2 Zinc white 2	Olive green 3 Cobalt blue 1

Special notes

Creating distance in tone

There are many ways of making your picture look as if it truly encompasses space and dimension. Sometimes you can use scale – the house that is farthest away is also the smallest; you can use colour, as on the next page; and you can use tone. The progressions on the right are a combination of tone, horizontal scale and vertical scale.

In the first progression on the right the blocks of sienna chalk appear to be receding towards the top of the page. The effect is created very simply by a change in tone from the darkest at the bottom to the palest at the top.

It is a good idea to make a few tone charts just like this and keep them tacked up in your studio. By and large, the use of dark, middle and light can be found in almost every kind of landscape; the foreground is almost always darker, heavier, brighter and generally also sharper in outline. Everything becomes more blurred and lighter as you move away.

In the two remaining charts, you can see the difference between horizontal progression and vertical progression. The strokes at the base of the centre column are thick and heavy. As the eye moves up, they become thinner, although they remain exactly the same height. Nonetheless, although the top strokes are just as long as the bottom – wider – ones, they seem to recede dramatically. Van Gogh frequently used this particular trick – horizontal progression – cutting reed pens to suit each progression in his paintings of farmland and growing crops.

The chart on the far right shows what happens when the lines remain the same width, but become shorter and shorter. In this – vertical progression – the sense of distance is just as strong.

These are all perfectly legitimate uses of real perspective, or, as it is technically known, aerial perspective. You don't have to work out sightlines or vanishing points. Simply put down what you see, in various ways.

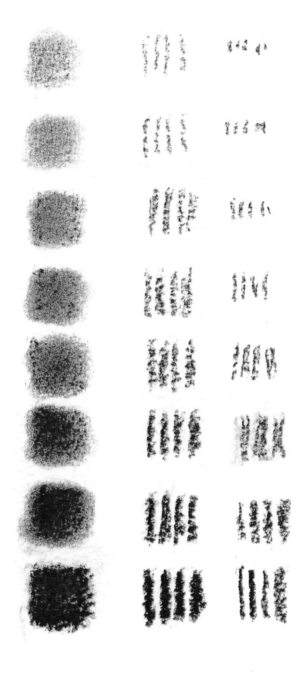

Creating distance in colour

In the previous groups of tonal patterns you saw how to make your landscape come near, or stretch out in the distance, without using any colour. On the opposite page there is an example of the same principle, but carried out in colour, and with very little use of line. Look at it carefully: a path through the woods, with the trees on the left gradually receding with the road towards some distant farmland.

Now look even more carefully. The diagonal path is actually not very diagonal – only the trees come down towards a vanishing point.

And if you drew around the outlines, the line of the path is so flat thay it wouldn't show up as receding at all.

But add the colour – strong ochre in front, gradually paling towards the horizon – and suddenly you have a natural progression. Make the point even more obvious with the dark trees, also receding towards a pale green blur, and you can see how easy it is to create space and dimension in the simplest picture. Most colours near us, in the foreground, are clear and bright. As we look away, the effect of the atmosphere and the sky is to cool down the colours and create a soft hazy outline.

People often say that a mountain in the distance looks quite close by when the air is clear and its outlines are crisp and sharp. This is also true of colour values. If we can see the deep blues and sharp greens of an alpine landscape, it will appear very near; fade the colour, blur the outline, and the mountain moves away.

Try this for yourself by making sketches of some distant scene. Pick out a church on a hill, or some distant feature of the landscape. In your first study depict the church in bold colours and standing out clearly against the sky. Then draw the same scene, perhaps in pastel or watercolour, with soft outlines using the broad side of the stick or a soft brush, in delicate colours of pale blue and purple. Distant horizons, indeed.

Bare branches

One of the pleasantest things about painting landscapes in
watercolour is how much you can do with very little. In the
little sketch on page 10, the paper was used without paint to
look like the trunks of trees. Although I did that by washing
around the faint pencil lines of the trunks, you can make it
even easier by using resist, a yellow fluid. Paint it on and let
it dry, then wash over, painting tree tops or whatever you
want. When the wash is completely dry, simply rub the resist
off with your fingers, leaving clean white spaces.

In this sketch of a woodland, I wanted to make much more
of the white clouds which left pale-coloured shadows
everywhere I looked. Resist would have left far too sharp an
edge, so I simply washed in the strongest areas, and left the
white paper to work for me in the ground and the sky.

Snow colours

It is remarkable how grimy everything seems when we see it in contrast to newly fallen snow. To be able to paint that glittering, glistening white seems an impossible task, but there are two hints that have proved useful to me out in the winter landscape.

The first is simply a matter of appreciating that there are a great many unexpected colours everywhere. This is especially true of snow scenes. We are conditioned to thinking of snow only in shades of white. But shadows, hollows and drifts of the snow itself are full of pale blues, ochres, greens, even pinks.

And those objects which at first you think are dark are actually much lighter than you realize; it is the contrast that throws them into relief. If you try to paint what you think you see, the scene will lose its brightness and sparkle.

So I always decide that the darkest object in the picture – whether it's a tree, a rock, or, as in this case, a fence-post – will not have any tone darker than mid-grey. Once I put in the mid-tones, all the other colours seem to rise to the surface. I never use black for anything except the faintest touches here and there to bring something into prominence.

The second hint is also based on tonal relationships. On a sunny day, when the snow and ice are really sparkling, you will find it difficult to paint in the highlights of frosted glitter which, in the words of the soap commercial, are whiter than white. Leaving the paper or canvas bare in this case will simply not be enough.

You must slightly pull down the tone of everything in the painting. Most of the snow itself should be painted in cream, as it is here; or you can try the palest blue, or even pink. All the other objects should be similarly keyed down, with not a speck of pure white anywhere.

Finally, after everything else is finished, take your thinnest paint brush, and with Chinese white in watercolour or titanium white in oil, create highlights wherever the sun makes the snow sparkle.

Stormy weather: sky painting

The sky is a major presence in most landscape painting, and sometimes, as in this storm-laden scene, it makes up something like eighty per cent of the picture. I suppose this might better be called a skyscape, with only the tops of the trees to create the impression of our being tied to the earth at all.

In this case, the storm was just above my head, and the horizon was gradually clearing. A first pale grey wash established the tonal base. An ochre wash was added to give that slightly greasy look which rain brings to the clouds. Then darker washes at the top were laid down in fairly broad undulating strokes.

At the end, while the last washes were still wet, I quickly put in the tops of the trees, so that their edges blurred slightly . That is the best way I have found to give a feeling of drenched foliage.

Try it for yourself. Look carefully out of the window the next time it is raining heavily, and you will see how your eye, peering through the curtain of water, will put rippled edges on everything.

This is a much more subtle way of painting rain than by marking the glinting edges of raindrops as they fall. It's important, with so little visible apart from the sky, that you accentuate the difference between the trees and the horizon by painting the treetops dramatically vertical. Instead of running a wavy line as I did in the summer landscape on page 32, I made sure that every brush-stroke began at the tree's top and moved down off the paper.

The stormy weather also affects the colour of the tree-line. You can see how much olive green is in the wash I used, with a fair proportion of lamp black. Lamp black is much warmer than the usual ivory black; it has a browny cast which was perfect for this weather.

Some stormy skies might be much cooler in tone than this. You have to observe what is happening in the sky and take note of how different kinds of storms create quite different situations. Sometimes the sunlight streaking through the rain makes wonderful bands of light – perhaps only lighter grey, perhaps tinged with yellow. At other times you may see rusty reds around the edges of the clouds, or ochres, or purples.

A good project would be to paint the sky from the same place every night for a week. Just make quick watercolour or oil sketches. I think you'll be astonished by the variety.

Trees

In most landscapes, whatever area isn't taken up by the sky is devoted to trees. There will probably be twenty or thirty different kinds within view of your easel.

How on earth can we convey the characteristics that make up each species, let alone the individual trees? One answer is by precise drawing. But when we are involved in painting landscapes, too much detail is not necessarily the best approach. Many painters might disagree with me, and artists of the nineteenth and early twentieth centuries delighted in painting genre scenes of gardens or landscapes, with every tree and shrub in crisp, almost microscopic, detail. While I admire their technique, I have no wish to suggest that you aim to achieve the same result.

Here are two entirely different approaches:

The oil opposite is almost an abstract of a tree. Close up, all you can see is the texture of the brush-strokes, and the colour; but in the finished painting, the tree emerges perfectly well. The little watercolour above is in complete contrast. It is based on silhouette and form, painted without any obvious texture and in a totally non-tree-like colour – a monochrome colour at that. Yet I believe that it, too, in the context of the drawing, works well.

A first approach:
the minimal landscape

These next three projects were planned to suggest ways in which landscape painting out of doors can give you both pleasure and a way of developing its craftsmanship. All of us, even the most experienced and dedicated artists, need times of complete relaxation and simple enjoyment.

For beginners who are making their first attempts at landscape painting, it is important to keep that feeling of freshness and pleasure alive even – or especially – through the difficult moments when the desire to achieve fights with a still limited ability.

So there should always be a place in your country outings for the minimal landscape. This is the occasion when you look at something for a few moments, and, before your mind gets crowded with planning, weighing up the possibilities, and working out the permutations, you simply put down the characteristics that jump out at you. The one line of the horizon, the one round ball of the evening sun – and there is your picture!

This does not necessarily mean minimal effort. It does mean looking for the fundamental images in front of you, and pulling those, and only those, out of the landscape and into your painting.

And it also means knowing when to stop. As soon as those first strokes are down, stop painting. Go for a cup of tea, walk about, have a picnic.

Whenever you are too wound up to concentrate, whenever you need a mental break from worrying about a picture that is simply not working, or whenever you want to wear your ambition to paint a little more lightly than usual, try something like this.

I should add that the bonus in such reduction to fundamentals can be a most beneficial effect on how you paint, no matter whether this eventually becomes your own personal style, or merely a way of putting down impressions for later re-working.

A second approach: abstracting the landscape

Once you have learned to distinguish the basic forms of the landscape from the covering of pretty greenery, you might enjoy trying one of the ways in which those forms are used to create still another style of painting, the abstract.

Abstract painting is by no means new. Many kinds of tribal art show the same interest in making forms and patterns out of realistic objects and emotional responses as does the work of modernists. But it does offer the landscape painter an alternative approach to form and colour that can be satisfying and productive.

I like to keep a strong link with the landscape itself, even when I use the sort of abstract imagery shown here. The hillside which was the inspiration for this painting had various fields in different stages – growing crops, lying fallow and so on. When I looked at the scene I could see that it would be relatively simple to heighten the colours, using much stronger and intense tones. The fields themselves inspired the pattern of rectangles; the curve of the hill marks the edge of the pattern.

Even if you think you don't enjoy looking at abstract art, it
makes sense to try this form yourself, if only to appreciate
how much is derived from everything we see. It was
Cézanne who said that all nature was a series of cones,
cylinders and rectangles. Many of his works, especially
scenes of the forest and clusters of buildings, in shades of
blue and dark green, are almost completely abstracted from
the landscape which we can see in his earlier paintings.
Remember always that abstract art is not an excuse for not
knowing how to paint. The attitude that you can simply slap
down a few semi-geometric shapes and give them a
significant title is out-of-date.

On the contrary, it takes creativity and a feeling for
atmosphere and place to see landscape in its underlying
blocks of colour and texture, to work with nature instead of
ignoring it.

If you enjoy this particular project, give yourself five or ten
minutes to make an abstract study on each of your painting
trips. Set them next to the other paintings, and see how they
compare, what essential images they caught, and which
subjects you feel succeeded best.

A third approach:
putting it all together

When you have been painting out in the country for a while,
you should give yourself a challenge to see how far you
have progressed, and in what direction your work is likely
to go. Now is the time to try something where there are
many different elements to weld together, and where you
need to control the composition, the colour and the texture.
Make sure you have a big enough canvas or paper, at least a
third larger than anything you have tried before. The
medium doesn't matter; the size does; it is easier to
manipulate the elements when you are working on a
reasonable scale.

The first goal is to make a number of sketches based on
tone, on colour and on the shapes you see. These will be

useful references throughout the project. It will take you at least a day, and perhaps as long as a week, to finish the painting, and the light and the shadows will change the look of everything from hour to hour.

The diagonal of the path shown offers good practice in perspective. The tree cast shadows which moved while I was there, making it necessary for me to refer to the sketches quite often, and the building just edging into view on the right added a strong geometric shape. It could equally have been the end of a barn, a tall columnar tree like a poplar, or even a large fence.

Take all the time you need, but make a note that you know what your capacity is. When you become truly serious about painting, keeping a diary of what you do and when can be a valuable asset in self-assessment.

Judging the results

To achieve the best that you can, you'll have to set yourself some goals, and learn to evaluate your own results. We can all be a little reluctant to push ourselves beyond what seems a comfortable degree of achievement; but in painting, as in any other part of our lives, the extra effort to reach just that little bit further will bring disproportionate rewards.

When you have settled into a routine of painting out of doors, you should give yourself a structure to help make the most of your time and to help you see what you've accomplished.

We've talked about planning ahead, looking about for subjects, being aware of what is available and so on. In order to use everything to the best advantage, and to achieve constant improvement, make up a working diary for all your outings.

Keep a note of where you go; what you see; whether you made sketches of preliminary compositions or painted straight on to the canvas; what colour range you used, and whether you found when you got home that it seemed too light or too dark ... Everything, in short, that will help you to judge how much potential you are utilizing.

For example, you can see opposite three little sketches of the same scene, but with the distance from the house growing less each time. It is the sort of process you should employ, before you start to paint, when you are still looking for the best composition or the most interesting point of view.

With a record like this in your diary, showing what you had to choose from, you can follow your own train of thought and, perhaps, remind yourself the next time to try one of the other possibilities, or to concentrate instead on the foreground or the middle ground until you can achieve better results.

Learning to be objective about yourself and what you can accomplish is one of the ways that painters turn into artists.

Index

Page numbers in *italic* refer to captions and illustrations.

Note on colour charts: the guides in this book have been produced within the limitations of four-colour process printing, and therefore cannot reflect the intensity of certain pure pigments.